SCRAPS

W. Grady Shope

SHOPE SHAK PUBLISHING

PO Box 7031, Asheville, NC 28802

www.shopeshak.com

"As told to Jenny Schermerhorn"

www.jennyschermerhorn.com

Editing by:

Farrell Sylvest

www.farrellsylvest.com

Photography by:

Colton Kilgore

www.kilgoreproductions.com

CONTENTS

THANK YOU

THANK YOU

This book would not have been possible without the selfless love of Sherri McCready. Her ability to be transparent and love strong in the storm amazes me. In my resistance to tell my story, Sherri would say, Grady, "You can't tell your story without telling your story." She spent hours listening to my stories, keeping me on track, saying "yes" and "amen", and pushing back with love. I think she could slap me and I'd thank her. I love you Sherri.

How do I thank all my friends who have been there for me through the storm? My family - you are one tough bunch and I'll always be ready to get in the fight for you.

A special thanks to my good friend Danny Hayes who encouraged me to get up again and discover that life wasn't over when you're fired.

My best friend, Kevin Gentry, who put his world on hold for months when my father died. He is a rock and continues to amaze me with his endless intelligence, perfectionism and attention to detail. Why do you want to hang out with an ole' redneck like me?

The hardest working man I know, Luke Miller. Thank you for displaying sacrificial love for your family. Even when your world was dark, you didn't quit. You kept going and showed me what love for family meant.

My childhood friend, Stefan "Steebo" Bonitz, who is the most incredible metal artist ever. We've taken different paths in life, but we've stayed connected and demonstrate what life long friends look like.

Many new friends have come into my life over the past seven years, like Greg Peniston. Most people wouldn't be seen in public with him, but I know he needs love too. Na! I'm joking! What a great guy!

My main man, Jazzion Cathcart, the mighty beast of God! This would be the man that would crack the stone wall for me in 2009. A man who didn't know my name, came up to me at a church retreat and said, "Can I wash your feet?" This man is the size of a dump truck and I was too scared to say no. The humbleness he displayed as he washed my feet would pierce my heart. Thank you, you big ole' dump truck!

Thanks to my favorite Super Star, Adam Copeland, for encouraging me to take care of my health and displaying over and over in his own life what it means to get up again. Through all of his injuries he overcame the impossible to fulfill his childhood dream and is still doing what is most important to him. "No" is a challenge to this man! Thanks buddy!

Finally, the sweetest woman I've ever met, Holly P. Fisher. This woman would love me through the whole storm. Even when she was bed ridden by her earthly disease, she continued to be an example of what grace, love, forgiveness and commitment to God looked like. Every Thursday night for years we would have dinner for two at her bedside. Her husband and my friend, Ray S. Fisher, would spend the whole evening preparing a meal for us. Thank you Holly for always showing me that even in the place of affliction, God still loved me. In my rights and wrongs, he's always there. What a God send to so many! I miss you!

Additional thanks to: Steph and Chuck Litchenburg, Pastor Tim Skinner, Andy Marthler, Eddie White, my FedEx Express Family, Jason Garris, Shannon McCready, Bryan Worthy, Colton Kilgore, Chris Lewis, Bryan Fore,

Doris "Grammy" Howard, Celia Thurman, Beth Kocianski, Anthony Byers, Jason Phillips, Danny Bishop, Norma Price, Pastor Norman Hardman, Alton Scott, Dr. Caldwell, Kim Scott, Josh Simpson, Jonathan Johnson, "JJ", Josh Phillips, Pastor James I. Walker, Peter Hobbs, Scott Criss, the Gutierrez Family, Kenny Holderman, David Patton, Eric Howie, Nate Huff, Patrick Scully, Paul "Smitty" Smith, Scott McCabe and all my "Leather Necks".

I spent hours at Greenlife, aka Whole Foods, sitting at a high top table with headphones plugged in as I attempted to find the right words to tell my story. I was also experiencing a lot of emotions which probably explained some of the looks I got from customers who must have thought, *there's really something wrong with that guy.* Thanks for serving the greatest coffee in WNC, Dynamite Coffee, Black Mountain, NC.

Love all of y'all!

SCRAPS

Seven Years

The worst train wreck ever.

Seven years ago I was standing at my dad's front door. I felt rejected and alone. I had been criticized in public, fired and told not to ever return to my former place of work which was also my church. "Don't call, don't email, don't come on the premises, get out." This was incredibly difficult to hear from the pastor, a man I served with for years. I was a broken man.

I had been "Pastor Grady," a part of the senior pastoral staff, ministering to families in the church, attending conferences, preaching at crusades and traveling to 23 countries to help in the building of orphanages. Suddenly I was standing in a void, empty of what had filled my life for years.

I deeply admired the senior pastor during my early years of serving the church community. Having great leadership and communication skills, he led a successful ministry and held long-term visions for the church. He was committed to building a strong ministerial staff.

1

I had been willing to do the most basic things for the senior pastor; even carrying bags and shining shoes. I thought I was serving God through any tasks asked of me and perhaps in a way it was a way of serving. My mistake was making the senior pastor into *God*. I take full responsibility for the confusion in my loyalty. Serving the church consumed my life and I didn't realize what I was doing to my family and friends.

The church became my new family and I completely shut out my dad and previous relationships. Church does become an extended family for many and rightfully so. At the time I didn't realize that I had taken this to a harmful extreme. I wouldn't spend holidays with my family; always choosing church commitments over spending time with them. My dad took a backseat in my life. He would say, "It can't be healthy for anything to consume your life to that level." I couldn't see it and even through his hurt, he still loved me.

It slowly became clear to me that something was unhealthy in the church I was serving. An observer might believe my life was going great but on the inside I was dying. Every time I wanted to move forward with an idea, the answer was *no* unless it supported the pastor's vision for the church. This seemed in complete contrast to the relationship I remembered my grandfather having with his fellow ministers.

When my grandfather went to Tennessee to preach revivals, segregation was still practiced. Dr. Wesley Grant, a black man, preached with my grandfather. My granddaddy was paid with canned food that filled the back of his car. When they returned to North Carolina, my grandfather would give half of the food to Dr. Grant to supplement the smaller portion he received because he was black. My grandfather knew that he could use more food because he had a larger family.

I began to think about how my granddaddy supported his fellow pastor, even sacrificing for him. He didn't put him down and in addition to sharing a portion of his pay, he went out of his way to bless and care for him. I wanted that kind of relationship with the church family I served. I wanted the church leadership to function in a loving and supportive way.

Everything came to a head one morning in a senior staff

meeting with about 14 attending. The pastor said he had something to discuss as he passed out pieces of paper. "This is a non-compete contract that I want all you guys to sign. It states that you can't start a church for two years within 200 miles of this city." I stood up and said that I wasn't willing to sign. It wasn't that I wanted to start another church; it was what the pastor communicated through his request.

I was raised in a church where we promoted and supported people in any ministry they felt called to do. Whether it was next door or a world away, if a person was called to serve, everyone was asking how they could help. They weren't concerned about territory, only supporting the person's call to ministry. I took a stand by leaving the meeting without signing the contract.

I asked my wife, worship leader at the church, to leave with me but she refused. I tried to share with her the spirit of dictatorship that I felt the senior pastor was creating. I reminded her that every time we approached him with dreams, like writing a book, recording a CD, even having children, the answer was always a strong *no*. He would not even allow us to travel overseas together. I felt like I was married to her *and* to him. She seemed unable to see the truth or to extricate herself from the situation.

As time passed, my anger grew, especially with the rumors that flew around me. In February of 2004, while holding a crusade in the Congo, I found out that the senior staff was planning to pull me off the mission field for a season. I tried to contact my wife several times during the trip but she never answered.

I felt that the leadership was blocking me from being obedient to my call to ministry and it was painful. A deep anger grew inside of me that I allowed to take over. I became vindictive and focused my rage on the senior pastor. I wish I had realized that I was falling into the devil's trap! I was feeling God calling me to leave but I was in too deep to just walk away. Instead of obeying the call to leave and protect my family, my character and my soul, I stayed and fed the anger already filling me. I kept telling myself, "It's me against them," as I allowed my anger to take over as I listened to the wrong voice.

I became a different person. I went from a person who was passionate about people, missions and seeing new believers becoming a part of the Body of Christ, to feeling like I had to watch my back. I was defensive and suspicious. I tried to talk to others in the church about my situation but the response was always, "You're being rebellious and out of the will of God." This was always the phrase spoken to anyone who left the church. I thought seriously about many others who had chosen to leave the church with similar reactions to the one I was receiving. I had often wondered, "When did we, the church, obtain the power to define God's will for other people?" Because this was now happening to me, I understood what so many others before me must have felt. They too were criticized and rejected because they dared to question the dictates of this particular ministry.

I will always remember the day I confronted the senior pastor. I asked him to allow me to continue on the mission field and he refused. I busted out his door, packed my things and left. I felt betrayed by the pastor and by my wife. Things got worse before they got better. I decided I would do everything I could to tear the church apart. I'm ashamed of the destructive path that I chose. I began to have a relationship with another woman who would feed me information about the church for the next four months.

I'll never forget the day I realized what a mess I'd made of my life and ministry. I felt like I'd ruined everything. I was staying at this woman's house and I felt the Holy Spirit pointing out my sin and telling me to run. So I did. I packed my clothes in trash bags, put them in the back of my pickup and left that night.

Once the senior pastor understood that I was really gone because I wouldn't agree to his demand to sign a non-compete agreement, he expelled me. A chapter in my life suddenly ended. Feeling that I had no self-worth, for days I contemplated suicide. I no longer had any pride. When I was able to admit that I was hungry, broken, lonely and empty, I drove to my dad's house.

I showed up at 7 am in the morning with 13 trash bags of my possessions stowed in the back of my truck. When my dad opened the door, tears immediately filled his eyes. He said, "Son, God woke me up at 3 o'clock this morning and I was on my knees pleading for your life." I tried to speak but nothing came out. "Don't say a word; welcome home Son." The word *son* became the most beautiful word in the world at that moment. I fell into my dad's acceptance and care and entered his home with joy.

For the next several days I mourned everything I had lost. I didn't eat; I cried and slept. Three days later when I pulled out of the fog, I found that my dad had emptied the 13 trash bags he found in my truck, washed everything and cleaned up my '91 Chevrolet pickup.

I sat down with my dad over a lunch he prepared. It was the best can of soup and grilled cheese sandwich I had ever eaten. I asked my dad to forgive me for turning my back on him and for making my service to the church my *God*. "I know, my son; I prayed you would see yourself as God saw you and come around." I had no home, job, ministry or money. "It's all ok Son; you'll get all that back and then some. First, you've got to let go of the mess you're dealing with. You were used like a yo-yo and made out to be the bad guy. God will have his moment with them. As for you, 'let your success be your revenge.'"

My dad was my hero that week and he wouldn't let me leave. With such tender kindness, he said, "I think you need to hang your hat here for awhile." I got a taste of what the Prodigal Son must have felt when his father ran out to meet him after all of his meanness, squandering and failure: unconditional acceptance and love, so undeserved and desperately needed. When I showed up on my dad's door step, feeling rejected, in great despair and smelling to high heaven, my daddy stood there and his expression said, underneath all that smell and funk, is "MY SON!" That is true love and fatherhood.

My dad made sacrifices to support me through the next months and years. I'll probably never know how much he gave up. I got a little glimpse about two years after he invited me to move in with him. On Sundays, my dad would go to JJ's house to watch the race and did so every Sunday for two years. I thought JJ was a guy and found out later that JJ was his girlfriend. The same week I showed up on his doorstep, he and JJ had been discussing selling his house and getting married. He changed his plans for me. He told JJ, "I'm going to stay with Grady through this because he needs me right now. I'm going to stay here until my son is better."

He put aside his own plans for his life to support me. I found out about his interrupted plans when he came to me and said that he felt it was a good time for him to leave because I was better, having healed from everything that happened. "I want you to buy this house, Son." I remember thinking, "No, I don't want this house, it's outdated and why would he move?" When I told him I didn't want the house, he smiled and said, "I'll give you three days to think about it."

Sometimes a daddy knows what you need. The house might feel out-dated and ill-fitting but now I realized he'd given me a home. I was humbled when I found out he stayed for me, delaying his plans to marry JJ after I showed up on his doorstep years ago. He died before he could marry JJ and I will always remember the sacrifices he made for me. I did buy my dad's home and what I thought was outdated is now filled with his love and sacrifice, the true meaning of service.

The Scraps

A marriage, a ministry, a job; ended, gone. Overnight my life was altered at the deepest levels.

Trying to clear my mind, I hung out in coffee shops and hiked a lot. It was hard to go out in public settings because I felt like people were staring and talking about me. I wasn't ready to encounter co-workers or church members. Confusion and uncertainty clouded my mind. I had served in the military and then trained for church ministry. I wasn't ready to look for another job in ministry so I tried to do freelance graphic design work but my ADD made it difficult to sit and look at a screen all day.

The shame and hurt I felt was unbearable, and I often thought about leaving Asheville. The idea of leaving and starting over was deeply appealing. I was seriously contemplating suicide because my life seemed so terrible and hopeless. I felt I had failed myself and everyone I cared about. I've fallen so far, even God can't redeem my circumstances. Sitting at a coffee shop, I wrote my son and my mom and dad goodbye letters. I printed the letters and left one at the house for my mom and dad. I hid my son's letter in a box full of stuff that I intended for him to have.

I was planning my exit. My parents discovered my letters earlier than I intended and I came home one day to find my mom and dad sitting in the living room waiting for me. They had tears in their eyes. My dad spoke first, "Son, sit down."

I sat on the arm of the couch. My dad knelt down slowly beside me and looked up at me, "Son, I want to show you something." He removed his watch, rolled up his sleeves, "Look here." I noticed scars on both of his wrists that I'd never seen before. My dad went on to explain that when he was 33 years old he tried to kill himself. He told me how despondent he felt after losing multiple businesses as a result of a messy divorce. One day he went home and cut both of his wrists. His sister somehow felt compelled to check on him, found him and saved his life.

His voice was shaking as he passionately told his story. "Suicide is one of the most selfish acts you can commit. You might just want to hurt yourself but you're going to destroy a son who loves you and a mom and dad who think you're incredible. Son, your world looks bad today but it'll change. Your pain may endure for a night but *joy* comes in the morning." The fact that he called me *Son*, and the truth that this would be a selfish act broke through my feelings of hopelessness. We huddled together in the living room, crying and hugging each other. It was the first time I had seen my dad display that much emotion. I never gave my son the box with the letter.

At that moment I knew that I should stay in Asheville and figure things out. I began to look for some sort of employment. After two months of filling out applications, FedEx offered me a job and as I look back, I know that the job offer was a provision from God. It was the best thing that could have happened to me at that time in my life. FedEx is fast paced, keeping your mind busy all day as you are loading packages, driving the truck and looking for the next stop while trying to beat the clock. It was like a game for me. I was delivering packages way out in the highlands of WNC and putting in 12 hour days.

The FedEx team took me in like family and during the short time I was there, I met some of the greatest people. We joked around all day and I enjoyed working alongside some other former Marines and a few Navy guys but more importantly to me, the manager, Gary Frady was a believer and a huge encouragement to me. Fred Smith, former Marine, the owner of FedEx, ran his company like a military operation and held everyone to a standard of excellence. Gary and I had conversations about God and he encouraged me often, reminding me that God would meet me wherever I was. He wanted me to go through the management program but before I could begin the program, new doors were opening for me in the construction field.

Seven months passed. It was still difficult at times, but I was getting better. Being alone with my thoughts was still difficult as I continued to reflect on my failures and everything I had lost. I slowly began to feel God's presence and His deep love for me.

A prominent pastor in the area, the senior pastor at Biltmore Baptist Church, James I. Walker met with me. He knew my father. He tried to become a mediator between me and my former pastor. He also tried to help me reconcile my marriage. Sadly, neither party was willing to meet. Pastor Walker encouraged me to get involved in a local church. He told me of a church that was just about to open at the Orange Peel in Asheville and that it might be a good fit for me.

It was a great fit but I still struggled with feeling worthless. I couldn't imagine anyone wanting to meet or talk with me. I would arrive at church late and leave early to avoid the pressure of engaging with anyone. I am so thankful that Pastor Walker saw through my brokenness and treated me like a person of value. The world might look through people but God sees value in us even when we can't see it ourselves. God ordained Pastor Walker to see my God-given value and he sent me to a place where others could see it too.

My Sin & Anger

I acknowledged my poor choices and took responsibility for them. I knew I wasn't the victim in this story. I began to see how harmful and unjust it is when a church turns its back on the imperfections in people. I am not anti-church and I became active in a church and was attending regularly. I do think that sometimes man gets in the way of God's plan for the church.

I realized how much I had lost touch with God's plan in the

midst of my hurt and anger after my mentor turned his back on me. The Marine in me laid into my fellow staff at that church. All that vindictiveness and anger ended up hurting me much more than it hurt them.

It tore me up to realize that I experienced the same treatment that I had participated in giving others by abandoning anyone who didn't do exactly as we said, making them believe they were outside the will of God. When people behave out of a dictatorship, they insist that you can't play in *their* sandbox. Only now from a distance could I clearly see that we were condemning God's people by placing judgments on their choices. Like the bully on the playground who is never wrong, when you leave the church you're seen as rebellious. Maybe it's not a sandbox after all, but a litter box.

Chosen

God's hand in my life has been apparent to me from my very beginning. I am thankful for the stories that my parents passed down to me. My mother was five months pregnant when she went to the hospital for a routine checkup. The doctor informed her that the baby was on its way. My mom was just 20 years old, frightened and confused. She agreed to have labor induced. What she didn't know was that the doctor had mistaken her for someone else. She took the small pills and began her labor that shouldn't have started for another 16 weeks. I arrived four months early weighing only 2 lbs. 2 oz. and was black and blue. I had no hair or finger nails or toe nails. They immediately removed me from my mother and put me in an incubator.

My dad remembers a phone call he made to his father from a pay-phone in the hospital hallway. "I don't think he's going to make it dad." My grandfather encouraged him, "He's going to be fine son. He has been *called* and he will carry my name. Don't worry about that one, he's called." My grandfather was certain of God's hand in this dark moment. He comforted my dad, as he was certain not only that I would live but that God had called me to ministry. I'm so proud to have a heritage of men in my family who love and trust in the Lord.

It would be three days before my mom or dad would be allowed to see me and thirty days until I was released from the hospital. I gained one pound a month after my birth and I've been gaining weight ever since! My mother spent eight hours a day with me until they released me to go home. I am deeply thankful to have been loved so well by my family through the care and attention they gave me from the very start.

Fast-forward 13 years

I felt a call to ministry when I was a skateboarding 13 year old boy. I was saved at Ben Lippen Bible Camp in Asheville, NC. I was invited by Mrs. Wright, a classy, godly woman in her sixties who attended a local church and taught high school typing at Reynolds High School. She was a grandmotherly woman, very sweet and nurturing. She held a Bible study group after school at Reynolds where my sister attended. My sister was never very interested but Mrs. Wright was kind and persistent. Eventually Mrs. Wright extended her interest beyond my sister to include me and would come by and pick me up every Sunday evening for services. I remember sitting in the back seat of her ancient car. It was neat as a pin inside with plastic covering the seats. I remember thinking I was going to sit down one day and be stuck permanently to those sticky plastic seats.

One summer she invited me to go to Ben Lippen Camp for a week. A young 13 year old, I found myself bunking with older teenagers in a building called the Squirrels Nest. It looked like an old military barrack. The *nest* had metal bunk beds that squeaked terribly and there was no bathroom. None of that mattered to me as I was delighted to be with the older kids. In one of the evening services that consisted of singing and preaching, I was convicted of my sin and deeply felt my need for God. I gave my soul over to Him. I came home from the camp with a certainty that something important had changed; I believed that I was called to preach.

I had a King James Version of the Bible which was all but unintelligible to me. I stuck to the Gospels; Matthew, Mark, Luke and John because honestly, I couldn't make sense of the other parts of the Bible. I used to wrestle my six foot wide wooden dresser mirror off my dresser, stand it upright and preach from the Gospels.

One Sunday after church as I was preaching, I looked into the mirror expecting to see myself and saw thousands of other faces; a huge crowd of black faces looking back at me. I fell on the floor crying and my mom ran in to check on me. She rushed into my bedroom and cried out, "What's wrong with you?" When I didn't respond, she yelled, "Are you on some kind of drugs?"

I laugh about this exchange now as it seemed like such a strange combination of truth and confusion. For years I wondered what that vision in the mirror had been. I knew I hadn't imagined it and hadn't been on any type of mind altering substances, so what did the image mean?

Call Confirmed

Fast forward twenty years and you'll find me at 5,150 feet above sea level in Dilla, Ethiopia. It didn't take much hiking at that elevation to be out of breath. Sometimes I just had to stand still for awhile to catch my breath. I was in Ethiopia with a group of men from my church to preach at a crusade. It took us several days of traveling to reach the town where we were expected. As we crested a hill after hiking up a winding trail through the mountains, we arrived at a huge clearing packed with people and what seemed to be an entire city constructed of banana leaves. The greens and browns of the landscape against the brilliant blue of the sky created one of the lushest environments I have ever experienced.

We held a three day crusade with an audience of about

30,000. We took shifts as we preached 24 hours a day. We were hoarse and happy, praising God for the interest that our audience brought to the crusade. The morning that I left, one of the main tribes who helped organize the crusade gave me their tribal drum as a gift. I felt humbled as I stood there holding the drum, looking out at the crowd of faces watching the presentation. That is when it hit me; this was the image I saw that day at the age of 13 as I looked into the wavy mirror.

I felt so secure. I felt certain of my call and so very blessed. It now makes sense to me why my experience at the church felt so gut-wrenching. I had been removed from a ministry that I felt called to serve. When I left the church, I didn't feel like I had only lost my job, I felt I had also been stripped of my calling. I've since learned that God's purposes for us are not always as narrow or as tied to a certain job or location as we might imagine.

Called For Life

I am a former Marine. When you join the Marines you're sent to Parris Island for boot camp. On the first day they're screaming at you and calling you every name in the book except your own and you wonder why you agreed to come.

You start to think that you might have messed up on this decision that felt so right at the time. The feeling I was having on the first day at boot camp was the same feeling I had after I was fired. I thought I misunderstood what God wanted me to do.

You're not allowed to refer to yourself as a Marine in boot camp; only a recruit. You're not a Marine until you march across the stage. Sixteen weeks after I started boot camp, I walked across the parade deck in my dress blues and became a United States Marine. Once you're a Marine, you're always a Marine. Marines don't refer to themselves as *Ex-Marine* and will only say *former Marine* if forced to. The honor, loyalty and grit required to be a Marine doesn't leave you even after your time ends as an official member of the military. It stays with you forever.

I've now come to see God's call in my life in the same way. It doesn't go away. God created me for a purpose and called me to serve Him. I will be serving, one way or another, forever.

I got off-balance for a while, confused by circumstances and emotions. I've learned to put my trust in the One who called me and I believe that He is powerful enough to use a sinner like me for His purposes.

Don't forget; God doesn't turn His back on the needy or the sinner as they are the people He has come to save. I rejoice that God is a God that loves and uses the leftovers, the *scraps*, for His good purposes.

Using the Scraps

Remember the story in John 6 where we read about Jesus feeding the five thousand? Something that happened after the miracle strikes me:

John 6: 12-13

"When the people had eaten their fill, he said to his disciples, "Gather the leftovers so nothing is wasted." They went to work and filled twelve large baskets with leftovers from the five barley loaves."

When he told the disciples to pick up the scraps, I'm sure they thought, why? We just fed over 5,000 people and they're satisfied so why does he want the scraps? He doesn't need them. He can always make more food! He's just proven that! I think it's because God doesn't waste anything. God's way of doing things is that He often chooses to use the foolish, weak, lowly and despised. Listen to what Paul says in 1 Corinthians about who God uses.

1 Corinthians 1: 26-31

26-31 Take a good look, friends, at who you were when you got called into this life. I don't see many of "the brightest and the best" among you, not many influential, not many from high-society families. Isn't it obvious that God deliberately chose men and women that the culture overlooks, exploits and abuses; choosing those "nobodies" to expose the hollow pretensions of the "somebody's?" That makes it quite clear that none of you can get by with blowing your own horn before God. Everything that we have—right thinking and right living, a clean slate and a fresh start—comes from God by way of Jesus Christ. That's why we have the saying, "If you're going to blow a horn, blow a trumpet for God."

I think the church often throws out the scraps because they are confused by their own pride and self-righteousness. They feel like they are following all the rules and feel threatened when others' lives are too messy, broken or different. So many people are running around hurt and lost, thinking God doesn't love them. "I've failed. I don't measure up. My dreams don't matter." The church fosters a limited view of Christ's followers because, through grace, no one is excluded.

The God I serve isn't a God who condemns, pushes away and scoffs. He is a God who seeks out the broken and offers restoration and reconciliation at a great personal cost. God is the *real daddy*. I am living in the peace of knowing that I am loved by God and accept His plans for me. My dad would say, "Son, if you're breathing the air of this world, God's not finished with you! *That'll preach!*"

People too often focus on what God says you *can't* do. I want to tell you what God *can* do. God can restore you, your marriage, your broken relationships and your ministry. Don't give up! If the church is more focused on who they won't let in and not focused on the healing that God offers the broken, it's not church yet!

God has reached down to the gates of hell and said, *those are my scraps; I want him, brush him off, clean him up. He is my child!* When you're a child of God, you're His child when you're a drug addict, adulteress, failed, weak, lost or crazy. No matter your circumstance in life, you still reside in the grace of the most high God!

Sham Authority

I was a slave without knowing it. I was serving the wrong people and believing false ideas about the true meaning of church. I was living with a focus on law; how things *should* be done and thinking my good deeds would earn me things from God. On the outside my life looked perfect. On the inside I was dying. I realized I was confusing being obedient with earning salvation. I was serving the wrong god.

Colossians 2: 11-15

11-15 Entering into this fullness is not something you figure out or achieve. It's not a matter of being circumcised or keeping a long list of laws. No, you're already in—insiders—not through some secretive initiation rite but rather through what Christ has already gone through for you, destroying the power of sin. If it's an initiation ritual you're after, you've already been through it by submitting to baptism. Going under the water was a burial of your old life; coming up out of it was a resurrection, God raising you from the dead as he did Christ. When you were stuck in your old sin-dead life, you were incapable of responding to God. God brought you alive—right along with Christ! Think of it! All sins forgiven, the slate wiped clean, that old arrest warrant canceled and nailed to Christ's cross. He stripped all the spiritual tyrants in the universe of their sham authority at the Cross and marched them naked through the streets.

Praise God that when he was nailed to the cross, our sin was also nailed to the cross!

There are thousands and thousands of people searching for God, running lost, looking for a Daddy, looking for a Church to love them and looking for someone to see the real person; for someone to see past their sin.

I'm amazed that even in my sin, God still wants to love me and still has a plan for me. I want to grab hold of, and for others to grab hold of this truth and not accept anything counterfeit that is presented as the truth.

Counterfeit purses look good from a distance but up close they don't measure up. The materials, the design; it's not the real thing. Don't accept some law-centered, counterfeit gospel. The real Gospel is too incredible to pass up: the God of the universe offering His love and care for sinners. God made you. He loves you. He wants you to run to Him and accept the gift of His love. Don't let anyone steal the truth and hand you a substitute!

I am living in the freedom of the Gospel and rejoicing that God's call on my life is not connected to human approval, job circumstances or a perfect record. He's picking up the scraps and getting me ready for what's to come.

Jeremiah 33:3
"Call to me and I will answer you. I'll tell you marvelous and wondrous things that you could never figure out on your own."

Put your *iphone* down and Call on **him.**

Affliction

When we suffer affliction during the hard times in our lives, we can encounter the love and grace of God.

My parents bought me a brand new black and yellow BMX bike with mag wheels. I was 11 at the time and could not have been more proud of my new bike! I decided I was going to take it down *the hill* by my house. *The hill* was known to all the kids in the neighborhood as the most fun and dangerous spot for bikes. As I was working up my nerve to go for it, little did I know that Randy, the neighborhood bully, was planning a surprise.

Randy was sixteen, skinny and fast from running track in school and known for his frequent schemes directed toward the younger kids in the neighborhood.

As I muster my courage and take off down the hill, I'm thinking, "I've got this great bike, looking cool with my hair blowing back and I've conquered my fear." I'm about halfway down the hill when Randy jumped out from behind a tree and screamed, "SNAKE!" As the front wheel turned sideways I went over the handlebars and slid across the pavement on my chest and shoulder. Road rash covered my shoulders, chest and legs. I left my bike and limped home crying. My older sister took one look at me, "Why are you bleeding and crying?" She had a wary look in her eye that changed to anger when I told her what happened.

When I finished telling my sister what happened, she dashed out the front door screaming his name. She was quickly gaining on him when he took off running and managed to make it inside his house before she could catch him. When she got there she began beating on the door but of course he wouldn't come out. I'm still crying in pain as I stand in the street hearing my sister screaming, "I'll get you buddy!" I was astounded and delighted by the protective vengeance my sister was prepared to release on Randy.

The next day my mom gets a call from the principle. "Mrs. Shope, you need to come get your daughter because she beat up some guy and shoved him in a locker."

I may have been afflicted by Randy but I got to experience the fierce love of my sister.

Called to Rest

Affliction will make you want to open up a 55 gallon drum of whoop-@#$%! on somebody but I learned that the fight isn't in the flesh; it's in the spirit. You want to fight with the people who are up in your face but sometimes you have to understand that there is big stuff going on *behind the scenes* and God is calling you to rest in Him and battle in prayer.

Ephesians 6:12

"For our struggle is not against flesh and blood, but against the rulers, against the authorities, against the powers of this dark world and against the spiritual forces of evil in the heavenly realms."

When my troubles started in the church, I went off the deep end. They wanted me to fight and lose control. As they taunted me, I felt God telling me to *be still.* "They want you to fail, Grady. Stop! You'll fight this one on your knees, in your closet, with worship and with the ultimate weapon, his Word. "

Ephesians 6:13-17

[13]Be prepared. You're up against far more than you can handle on your own. Take all the help you can get, every weapon God has issued, so that when it's all over but the shouting you'll still be on your feet.

*Truth, righteousness, peace, faith, and salvation are more than words.
Learn how to apply them. You'll need them throughout your life.
God's Word is an indispensable weapon. In the same way, prayer is
essential in this ongoing warfare. Pray hard and long. Pray for your
brothers and sisters."*

When I finally understood that God was calling me to be
still and spend my energy on prayer instead of conflict,
things got very clear for me and very confusing for them.
They didn't know what to do when I stopped fighting.
People approached me to tell me that my old church was
falling apart and they wanted me to reengage. To their
request I would reply, "Sorry; I need to work on my own
sin, my own problems and let God handle that situation." I
felt such freedom in knowing that I was not in this conflict
alone and that God was offering me grace and calling me to
prayer and obedience.

When people repeatedly tried to get me to engage in
conversations about the church and my problems with the
church, I refused. As my dad said to me so many times,
"Silence is your greatest weapon."

I think of the movie Top Gun, where Maverick was dealing with the death of his co-pilot, Goose. His flight instructor was insisting Maverick get back into the sky. Maverick would go up but wouldn't engage in any of the training fights. He wasn't ready and his new co-pilot, Merlin was getting frustrated with him but Maverick refused to fight.

Take those *God is my co-pilot* bumper stickers off your cars, people. God isn't our co-pilot! He **IS** our pilot. He is in control. He needs to be guiding and directing our lives. We think we should engage and fight when we're afflicted but there's a healing process that we must undergo and if and when it is best for us, God will put us back in the fight.

My failure was still so fresh that I was still grieving and mourning my loss. It was like death. My father said the worst pain you can endure in life, outside of the loss of a loved one, is a divorce. I was suffering with that pain. I was enduring a divorce from my wife and my ministry. I think death might have even been easier to deal with because it is final. Your loved ones are still present in a divorce but lost to you. You still run into them and their friends and instead of being a loved one, you are now an object of disapproval and distaste.

I gave up fighting back and my hurts became scars. Healing took place but the impact and memories remained. Time passed and as I slowly made peace with my scars, things settled down. I purchased the home I grew up in, got married and moved forward with life.

Fresh Loss

I received a call in November 2008, that my dad was in the emergency room. I immediately rushed to the hospital. Fluid was accumulating around his heart and the doctor wanted to admit him for observation. I remember asking him, "Are you ok Pops?" He answered with, "Yeah man, just turn those bells off." The beeping of the heart monitor was annoying him.

They released him from the hospital after a few days and he said he felt great. He had a few follow-up doctors' appointments and assured us that everything was ok. I would hang out with him and carry firewood in the house because he loved a good fire. I bought a new truck in December 2008, and was excited to show it to him. I went to his house and he leaned up against his car, "Son, that's a truck right there. I'm so proud of you. You're building new homes, working on commercial buildings and making a new life for yourself. You got a great woman." He'd always tell me, "Nothing better than a good woman, nothing worst than a bad one."

A procedure was scheduled for December 23. He checked in on the 22nd and all was good for pre-op. I went to chat with my dad and we had some really good conversations for about four hours. I asked him so many things about his life. I wondered out loud if he had any regrets. I believed he had some regrets but he wasn't going to talk about them. He felt it was all water under the bridge. "I'm praying for Larry Jr." was the only thing he said to me. Larry Jr. is my older half brother, a man the size of a dump truck.

I've always looked up to Larry Jr. He was around a lot in my teens. He was funny, a little reckless and a great big brother. He worked for dad driving a semi-truck for a time. His CB handle was *three legged dog*. I spent many summers riding in the cab with him and unloading boxes of baby food in the muggy southern heat. Out of all the children, my dad worried about him the most. My brother was a *little sideways* at times. Being a little rowdy and a little redneck, Jr. could always find trouble. He had a temper and you didn't want to be around him when it went off. He was also not a believer and my dad worried he would die without confessing to Jesus. My dad prayed for him often. The other side of Larry Jr. is that he would always reach out to help others. I've seen my brother lay in mud puddles to change someone's tire. He would get in the trenches with anyone who needed help. My dad talked a lot that night about him and my sister Tina.

Today my brother and his family are a part of an incredible church and following Christ. He is now an example of not just being a great brother but a great father as well. His children and grandchildren are thick as thieves. The changes he's made in his life make me believe that prayer does work. My dad and I really didn't talk much about me that night and that was a good thing. I knew if we were talking about me that I must be doing something stupid! I hugged him goodbye and went home about 11:30 pm.

The next morning was the scheduled procedure but they felt he needed to wait till the 26th so he had to spend Christmas in the hospital.

On Christmas Day my family went to see him. He was cracking jokes and laughing, just being himself. He seemed to be in good spirits when we left to go our own ways. My son and I decided to go back to the hospital later that night. When we arrived we found him still awake, teasing and flirting with the nurses.

We stayed for an hour. When we left, his girlfriend, JJ followed me into the hallway and said, "Your dad isn't doing well." She was really worried. I told her I would be back in the morning and we hoped that the procedure would help.

The next morning I got to the hospital around 8 am and went to his room. My stomach dropped when I saw that his room was empty. The room was already clean and completely empty of any of my dad's things. I anxiously asked the hospital staff at the nurses' station, "Where's my dad?" They told me he had been sent to the ICU for his procedure.

I felt better about that but wasn't sure why he had been sent to the ICU. I managed to find the ICU and when I got there, found JJ in the waiting room. As soon as I entered the waiting room she began to cry, "Your dad isn't doing well." "Is this it? Is it over?" I asked. "I think so Grady." I sat down on the floor trying to gather my thoughts. I called my wife and told her to come quickly. "I'm going to see my dad whether they'll allow it or not. Get up here; they may lock me up once I'm done."

I left the waiting room, peered through a set of double doors and could see my dad lying on a bed. I saw his cardiologist and then saw a chaplain. Having served as clergy for a hospital, I knew what his presence meant. I began to pound on the door and ring the doorbell. The cardiologist motioned me in. The doctor told me that they were going to try the procedure and that my dad was aware that he was not doing well. My wife walked into the room just as my dad grabbed my hand and with great strength pulled me down to talk to me. "If you're breathing the air of this world, God isn't finished with you. I love you Son!" Thirty seconds later bells began to sound and a team of people rushed in. My wife and I were crowded out as the curtain closed on my last view of my dad alive. They worked on him furiously but he was gone.

He was gone. I begin to cry and anger rose inside of me. My cheerleader, my best friend, my hero was gone. I went into the hallway and called my brother to tell him our daddy was gone. It was so hard to think he was dead. One of my best friends, Kevin Gentry, helped me get through the worst of my grief. He took time off from work to counsel me, came to the funeral, the wake and in the months to come would call or come pick me up to help me fill my time.

I've realized that affliction comes in many packages. Sometimes it's self-affliction and at other times it comes from outside sources that you have no control over. This was a deep hurt and I staggered under the weight of it. Every day was hard. I felt I had just recovered from one giant hurdle and now I struggled to accept that I had lost my dad.

"Time will pass," my aunt told me one day. "Your daddy was so proud of you, Grady. He would carry pictures of you in his pocket and show people the pictures from Africa and the houses you built." Those words brought me peace, even as they caused me pain. I'm so glad my dad answered the door that day. I believe it was worth all that I went through to get to see my Father's love for me.

Seven Years of Sanding

I work as a General Contractor. Sometimes my job includes

working on older, historical houses. I first meet with the owners to discuss what they need. "I don't know what to do with the floors in this house. As you can see, they have been painted many times over the years as each new owner chose yet another color."

I'll look at the floors as I take a knife and scrape the paint off. "Do you know what you have here? These are heart pine floors; the most expensive floors that you can have. People who reclaim lumber would almost die to get their hands on heart pine because you can't get it anymore." "You mean to tell me we can sand this down to the original heart pine?" "Yes, but the sanding process is extensive."

To get down to that beautiful heart pine floor, you have to start out with really tough 40 grit sandpaper and slowly work down to what is underneath. You take off the first layer and then using 60 grit sandpaper take off another layer. You slowly work down until you are using very fine 80 grit sandpaper. This slow process takes off the years of paint and grime to expose the original flooring without damaging it.

The last seven years of my life have been God sanding away

at my affliction. It hasn't felt good but he has used this grit to smooth away sin and I have felt Him saying, "What I have underneath is my son, my child."

New Beginnings

I am very happy with the new church family God has given me. The church God brought to my city is incredible. Highland Christian Church led by Pastor Shannon and Sherri McCready meets in a local music venue every Sunday. I attended Highland's very first service and I'm still there.

Even in my sin and my failures, they accepted me. I needed a true church; not one that would cast me out or one that would turn their back on me, but one that would take me as I am, willing to get in the trenches with me. To give a hand up, not a hand out! *That'll preach.*

I went to the pastor and told him my story, "If you do not want me in this church, I will understand." He said, "Church doesn't just need well people but the broken ones too." Shew!

I am so thankful for the pastor at this church. What an

incredible man of God. This man isn't just a pastor; he's a godly father, husband and friend. He's not looking for recognition for his *goodness,* but is making sacrifices to display the goodness of God, for the glory of God. Every Sunday, he says, "We are to change life as we know it, through the love, loyalty and friendship of Jesus Christ." He doesn't just believe it and say it, he lives it!

Five years after I failed at my ministry, my marriage, being a good daddy and a good friend, I was sitting in a coffee shop having a conversation with Pastor Shannon. I felt ready to offer my service to the church. I wasn't looking for something big, just a behind the scenes spot to stretch outside myself. I thought it was going to be a day of a small victory but it was going to be a painful day of the re-surfacing of an affliction. Often the source of our pain, our affliction will resurface multiple times. I didn't just deal with the loss of my ministry, my job and my family once but over and over again. It makes me think of Paul's *thorn in the flesh.* He couldn't get rid of that thing and he sure sounded tired of dealing with it!

Don't be surprised when something you thought you'd dealt with and put behind you shows up again. God won't abandon you. He's there and ready to help you in the pain, the loss, the confusion and frustration again and again.

So here I am, sitting in the coffee shop after 5 years of working on myself and trying to find forgiveness from those I hurt and those who hurt me. I felt like it was finally my day to move forward. Guess who walks into that very coffee shop on that cold winter day but my former pastor. I hadn't seen him since leaving his church and Pastor Shannon had never met him. I stood up when he passed by our table and introduced him to Pastor Shannon. It was awkward in that brief moment. He left and we continued our conversation.

It turns out he didn't leave but went to his car to wait for us to leave the coffee shop. With his voice shaking with passion, he told Pastor Shannon, "You'd better watch that man. He's dangerous, he needs counseling and he's crazy!"

I'm thankful that Pastor Shannon took his words with a large grain of salt because he knew me and knew enough about the situation to make the choice to trust me. I was grateful for his support even as I struggled with the re-emergence of a situation I hoped was long dead and gone.

Do you ever feel like the devil is waiting for you; waiting to pounce when you are just recovering from his last assault? Affliction will keep you on your toes, humble and broken. I think that's the reality of the world we live in but there is incredible hope because our God uses broken people. Listen to Paul's writing about his *handicap*:

2 Corinthians 12:7-10

7-10 Because of the extravagance of those revelations, and so I wouldn't get a big head, I was given the gift of a handicap to keep me in constant touch with my limitations. Satan's angel did his best to get me down; what he in fact did was push me to my knees. No danger then of walking around high and mighty! At first I didn't think of it as a gift, and begged God to remove it. Three times I did that, and then he told me, My grace is enough; it's all you need. My strength comes into its own in your weakness. Once I heard that, I was glad to let it happen. I quit focusing on the handicap and began appreciating the gift. It was a case of Christ's strength moving in on my weakness. Now I take limitations in stride, and with good cheer, these limitations that cut me down to size—abuse, accidents, opposition, bad breaks. I just let Christ take over! And so the weaker I get, the stronger I become.

Amen! It's been 7 years now since I went through my job

loss and I'm still dealing with pain, loss and character assaults. I've learned that in weakness, God can be strong. My Marine training kicks in when I think about this. I might be *low crawling* through the mud and barbwire, shot at, kicked in the face and told we won't win but the Marines don't quit. We'll just brush off the dust and come back for more. We were trained to be fighters, not quitters. The beauty of being a follower of Christ is that he doesn't call you to fight alone because He is with you. He offers to be your strength and shield as you go through life's battle.

Gen. William Thornson of the U.S. Army said, "There are only two kinds of people who understand Marines: Marines and the enemy. Everyone else has a second-hand opinion."

Being a former Marine taught me to focus on the fact that I serve the winning side. My God is sitting on the throne and He *will* be the Victor. No matter what my personal circumstances, I'm willing to suit up and follow Him wherever he takes me. Sometimes he takes me to some really uncomfortable, hard places.

I think I can better understand why David said, "It is good that I was afflicted."

This season of my life has brought me closer to God and deeper into His Word. For a time I wanted to run away from my troubles and get away from the pain; to once and for all, *get it all behind me.* Other circumstances found me wanting to fight and work-it-out. I found real peace when I took it all to God. I'm so thankful and amazed that God didn't allow me to be destroyed by my own poor choices and sin. He even used those circumstances to shape me into more of what He wanted me to be. When I became nothing, He became more to me. My affliction showed me His love for me.

Your Name

Your name is one of the first things in life that belongs to you. Your parents put some thought into your name while you were still in the womb. They considered a name that either holds significance because it was a family name or a name that holds special meaning because it belongs to someone who made an impact on them. They chose it for a reason. Even if you were named after a fruit, your name was chosen for you. If your name is apple, orange or Fred Flintstone, it is *your* name!

I was named after both of my grandfathers, James Grady Shope, my dad's father and William Varner on my mom's side. Even though I weighed in at just 2 lbs., I was given the big name, William Grady Shope. I never met William Varner and don't know much about him but I do know a lot about my granddaddy, James Grady.

Our last name, Shope, runs thick through these Blue Ridge Mountains. The Shope family has been here since the late 1800's. We've had a couple fly the coop but over all our people stayed local. That's a lil' that mountain talk for ya!

Every week I meet at least one person who hears my last name and asks me if I'm related to the Haw Creek Shopes. When I confirm I am part of that old clan, they launch into their own story. *Well my dad worked with your aunt . . . I remember meeting your grandfather . . .* Your name tethers you to something larger than yourself and Shope brings out stories and memories that go back for generations.

Side note: When I travel to New York City, people always ask me to talk for them. There is something about a southern boy's twang that those Northerners just love.

In the midst of a discussion about my last name, someone often asks, "Was James Grady your dad or grandfather?" I'm so proud to answer, "Yes." "Man, Grady, he could preach now. I remember him being in the middle of preaching and burst our singing, 'I'm climbing Jacob's ladder everyday, every rung goes higher and higher, I'm climbing Jacob's ladder everyday.' "

My grandfather, James Grady Shope died when I was 9 years old. Many of the things I know about him are from the memories of others. My Aunt Ruth Banks tells me that my grandfather was a wild man in his younger days. My grandmother was walking home from church through the woods one night when she heard a noise that she thought was a cow. It wasn't until the moaning turned into words that she knew it was a person, my grandfather, stone drunk and lying in the path. Folks would say that James Grady Shope would get so drunk that he'd lay in the curve on Riceville Road and dare cars to run over him.

My grandfather quit school in the 3rd grade because his father, Great Grandpa Harrison, needed both of his sons, James and Claude to help farm the head of Shope Creek.

When he got saved in 1933, he immediately began to preach with a focus on "amazing grace." He didn't have a Bible so he just preached to others what he heard himself.

As a young man, James Grady moved his family to Elizabethton, Tennessee to work at TVA as a heavy machine mechanic. They rented a nice brick home and the family enjoyed the security of a regular paycheck. Their security, however, turned out to be short-lived. My Aunt Ruth recalled the day Daddy walked in and told Mother he quit his job, "We're moving back to Asheville because God has called me to preach."

This story makes me laugh because it is so "Shope." None of us seems to be able to swallow punching a clock as we've found ways of making a living on our own.

So the young family moved back to Asheville and James Grady began building what he called "The Tabernacle." I don't know who owned the land, but I do know that he borrowed money from Mr. Buchanan, president of the bank in Swannanoa to secure the land and fund the building.

James Grady and two family friends, Norman Thomas and Fiz Garland, built the entire structure from rocks out of Shope Creek. They hauled the rocks out of the creek, loaded them on the back of an ancient flatbed truck and transported them six miles to the building site. An interesting note about the old flatbed truck is that one summer, James Grady took half of the residents of Grassy Branch to the beach on the back of that flat bed truck. From the walls to the water fountain, everything in the church building was constructed of rock. They used old wooden tent benches, used in tent revivals, for the pews. James Grady had the gift of faith. My Aunt Ruth remembers the time he prayed for a blind woman to be healed and her eyes were opened.

In 1954 Ralph Sexton, Sr. raised money for his "Jesus Saves Ministry" fund to be used for a mission in downtown Asheville. A tiny part of that money was used to buy my grandfather his first and only Bible.

Like many of the residents of Appalachia in the 1940's, my grandfather couldn't read or write. God did give him the ability to read his Bible. He would spend the rest of his life preaching the gospel, holding tent revivals and inspiring men and women to build the kingdom.

My grandfather purchased a white canvas revival tent for $400 and hauled it all over the mountains on that ole' flatbed truck. He'd set it up and start preaching. One time he erected the tent in Newport Tennessee and preached every night for three months and someone was saved each night. When he left, they gave him a "pounding." Back then people would give food instead of money as an honorarium and that came to be called a "pounding", gifts of baking ingredients like flour, sugar and cornmeal in one pound bags. It took three cars for him to haul it home. "I thought we were rich!" my aunt remembers.

God used my grandfather to minister to the people of Swannanoa Valley and his own family. It excites me to see how powerfully God used a man who couldn't read or write to make a huge impact on his community. We often think that we need to *be something* before God can use us. I'd rather think that God is just looking for open vessels to pour Himself through. You don't need to be perfect, just available. Love God and love people. It *IS* that simple.

Recently I met with my Aunt Ruth. As I was leaving, she said, "Come here little Grady." I'm not little but I'm the youngest of the Gradys in our family. I followed her into the home office. She leaned over and picked up an old Bible, lovingly dusted it off and said, "This is your Granddaddy's Bible. Granny Shope gave it to me when he died and I've had it for 32 years. When Granddad held you in his hands when you were just two months old and only three or four pounds, he looked up and said, 'This one will preach.' " "With so many things against you, I didn't know how you were going to make it when you were younger; so many things against you. I was worried. Now I'm saying take this Bible and go preach!"

That Bible is the greatest gift anyone has ever given me. I

will cherish it forever. I felt like I had been knighted by the Queen when my aunt gave me my Granddaddy's bible. It reminded me again of how powerfully our heritage can influence us. Here I was, holding my grandfather's Bible and feeling encouraged to share my brokenness and the faith that had healed me.

Your Name, Your Lineage

Your name is powerful. It is a part of you. Nobody can steal your name. People try to hurt others through the power of name-calling. It takes a lot of confidence and self-esteem to brush off the names that the world throws at us.

A husband telling his wife, "You're fat; you need to workout," then he wonders why she doesn't want to have sex with him. Yes man, I said it! Maybe what you need is a mirror, fool! She can fix fat, but you can't fix ugly. Call her by the names you used when you were trying to win her over, such as sweetie, baby or honey. Don't ask for the dessert after you've criticized the meal. *This will preach!*

I was a class clown since the first day they dropped me off at school. My kindergarten teacher was probably contacting the 12th grade staff to warn them to watch out for Grady

Shope. *It might be awhile, but he's coming.*

When I was in the sixth grade, my teacher, Mrs. Griffin would ask me almost every morning if I'd *like my licks now* because she was sure I was going to do something wrong before the day was out. I felt like my transgressions were worth the pain and it didn't matter how much my punishment hurt. I always entered the classroom smiling and that would get a round of laughter from my classmates. Poor Mrs. Griffin called my dad one day and said, "Grady needs to find something to do in the evenings to expel some of his energy."

My dad had many things that he tried to instill in us but one of his favorite sayings was, "There are two things in your life you don't want to ruin; one is your name and the other is your credit." Thanks to my dad's lessons, my credit is impeccable. I've found the real value of myself in the name that God calls me, *my Child.* Satan wants to steal this name from us and the world wants to label us with a multitude of names. Hold on to your identity in Christ; your "child of god" name. I'm not surprised that *Proverbs 18:21* says, "There is power in the tongue." There's life and death in what we say.

When I departed from my past, a man said to me, "You're nothing but Saul." I guess it appeared that way on the outside. I was trying to self-destruct. When people call you names, you can start believing those names. You start believing your name is Fat, Ugly, Loser, Failure, Adulteress, and Murderer and that you will never be anything but names given to you.

Well, I have news for you.

Romans 6:6
"Our old way of life was nailed to the cross with Christ, a decisive end to that sin-miserable life - - no longer at sin's every beck and call!"

Devil, you'd better learn my name! I'm a child of the most high God. Not a slave but a child. Being a child of His means that he is my Daddy. You can't label me worthless because I belong to Him.

I'm not Saul anymore because I'm taking back what has been stolen from me. David defeated the Amalekites with half the men. We're moving forward with that same help. We're not losing the battle because we are getting stronger. Sometimes when you're down you have to encourage yourself by acknowledging who we belong to and what that means. David had to encourage himself as we read in *1 Samuel 30:6, "David strengthened himself with trust in his God."*

The rest of the world may be tearing you apart and you might lose your swag and walk around with your head down. Don't listen to what others say. Know who you are and lift up your head. The devil knows who you are and that's why it's a fight.

Isaiah 43:1-4
"But now, God's Message,
> *the God who made you in the first place Jacob,*
> *the One who got you started, Israel:*
"Don't be afraid, I've redeemed you.
> ***I've called your name.** You're mine.*
When you're in over your head, I'll be there with you.
> *When you're in rough waters you will not go down.*
When you're between a rock and a hard place
> *It won't be a dead end*
Because I am God your personal God
> *The Holy of Israel your Savior.*
I paid a huge price for you;
> *All of Egypt, with rich Cush and Seba thrown in!*

That's how much you mean to me!
That's how much I love you!
I'd sell off the whole world to get you back,
Trade the creation just for you."

When we're drowning and sinking under all of the lies the world and the enemy tells us about ourselves, God reaches out his hand to rescue us. The next time the devil tries to change your name, escort that sucker right out the front door and tell him, "Next time you can address me by my name, *Child of God*. The only authority that the devil has is the authority we give him.

Take back your name. Just like my last name, Shope, evokes a deep heritage, stories, memories and connections, our *Child of God* name connects us to the power, love and care of our heavenly Father.

On his 18th birthday, my son called me and said, "I'm getting a tattoo." I groaned and smiled. I didn't allow him to get a tattoo while he lived at home. "That's a decision you need to make when you are an adult. Hold off for now." He was 18, away at college and was about to be *inked* so I drove out that afternoon to meet him at the tattoo parlor. I took *before* photos of his back and asked him what he was going to have done. "*SHOPE*," he said and in *BIG* letters. That boy had our last name written from one edge to the other on his broad tan back. It looked like he was wearing a sports jersey. He might be crazy but he understands the importance of name. He knows who he belongs to. He knows I'd do anything for him. He's my child and I want him to remember that as he makes his way in the world.

There's no Father without a Mother

Hard truth, pain, honor, forgiveness and love. These are words I think of when I reflect on my growing up years.

One thing for certain; you can change your friends but not your family. When I was a teenager, I said to my mother, "Please tell me I'm adopted or that you beat around the bush back in the day." She laughed and said, "No, that's your real daddy."

My dad hasn't always been the hero in my family. We laugh about it today, but it hurt during those years he was trying to find himself. My dad was wild; it's in our blood.

In 1970, my dad, Larry Shope, owned a restaurant, Larry's Chicken Hut, 110 pin ball machines located in bowling alleys and skating rinks and was District Manager for Liberty Life Insurance. He was very successful financially and his wild life would spend it for him.

My dad was in a hardware store one afternoon in Asheboro,

NC. He noticed a young woman, another customer, wearing a Kentucky Fried Chicken uniform. She was a little country girl who had been raised in an orphanage and hadn't finished the 9th grade. Her mother was struggling financially so she returned home to help with the raising of her younger brothers. She was one of 11 children with nine brothers and one sister. She was a hard worker, helping her mother and raising a five year old daughter of her own. She stood just five feet tall and was beautiful. My dad went up to her and said, "How would you like to come and work for me? I'll pay you double what you make at KFC." She agreed.

That young woman is my mother, Charlotte Jeanne Shope. My dad hired her to clean his house. On her first day, he drove her to his two story brick home and said, "Clean it up, tell me how long it takes and I'll pay you." He dropped her off and left. My mom remembers that day vividly. "I went in and discovered three women living in the house with him. It was disgusting, nasty and filthy. I have never been in a home so ill-kept."

Mom cleaned the house until it shined like a new penny. She gathered all of the women's clothing and stuffed them into trash bags. Larry was astonished when he returned home to see what Jeanne had done. "That little five foot of nothing turned that house back into a home," he once said. He told her to take the trash bags of clothes and the rest of the women's belongings and put them in the driveway. Then he had the locks changed. Bam. He moved those ole' dish rags out. He had already set his eyes on my mother and was ready to get serious no matter what it took.

So impressed with her hard work, he invited Jeanne out to dinner for a steak. Jeanne's parents, with eleven children to look after, sent her to a local orphanage because they couldn't afford to keep her fed and clothed. Having been raised in an orphanage, she had never seen or eaten a steak. In fact, she didn't even know what a steak was. When he invited her to go out to eat a steak, she responded, "You can't eat a stake; that's something you drive into the ground." My dad was confused at first but then he laughed. He took her out to dinner often and made sure she had everything she needed. A new life began for my mom. She saw a future that she never imagined for herself and her little girl.

One summer my parents drove to Myrtle Beach. My dad

loved cars and we drove down in a 1970 Dodge Challenger with a 426 HEMI. I was only one and with no car seat, my head was lolling around as I dozed in and out of sleep in the back. My dad was at the hotel sleeping one afternoon so my mom decided to take the car and go for a drive. When people rolled up to the red lights and noticed the car, they flirted with my mom and said, "Let's race, baby." She took them up on it. With me asleep in the back, my mom had a brief drag racing career. I laugh, especially knowing that she had to put a pillow behind her back in every car she drove just to be able to reach the pedals. She returned to the hotel room with $500 worth of tickets for drag racing on the strip.

My dad lost his businesses in 1971 and moved back to Asheville, NC. He had just enough money to purchase a Peterbilt Semi truck and begin his career as a truck driver. My mom was left at home a great deal of the time with a newborn and my 5 year old half-sister. She was confused by her new surroundings and would get lost going to the Laundromat just a mile from our house.

Truck drivers live a rough life; long hours on the road, temptations of available women and illegal drugs at truck stops. My dad's magnetic personality often got him into trouble. He had relationships with women up and down the eastern seaboard. His CB handle was *Tennessee Stud*. Really! "El-Studo," my cousins and family would call him.

My dad stayed on the road for three weeks at a time, come home, sleep for several days then start drinking Jack Daniels as soon as he woke up. He did have a drinking problem. My mom, trying to raise two children on her own and fit into a new community of people, started to feel as though she'd been rescued from one bad situation and ended up in a new one. Her new life was more polished because she had a car, furniture and a bit of money but the loneliness was still there.

My dad spent much of his time on the road and even when he was home, he wasn't present. My mom's emotional needs were not met, the house was in disrepair and the drinking was like pouring gasoline on his temper. He'd get drunk and then angry. My mom would confront him and then he would yell, often threatening to kick us out. It wasn't a hollow threat as we moved in and out four times before I was in the third grade.

Where's the man that met me at the front door on that day that I felt alone and rejected? I'll get to that but right now let me tell you about the most wonderful woman in the world, my mom. She never wavered or slumbered as a mother. She always found a way to make it work.

In 1977, my mom took a job at K-Mart where she worked for the next 30 years. That woman can commit to something. They hired her without a high school diploma which she still doesn't have today. She does have a *master's degree* in how to raise children and how to love and provide for a family.

I had a penchant for brand name clothes as a boy. I was desperate to fit in and be accepted by my classmates and knew that wearing certain clothes was one way to achieve this. My dad didn't think it was necessary for us to have brand names so he would only give my mom enough for functional jeans and shirts. My mom would take me to Ivy's at the mall. She would let me pick out one pair of jeans at a time and put them on layaway. She'd go back to the store and pay $5 every week until she paid them off. She got the money from her K-Mart job and did this for me all through elementary, middle and high school.

My mom was always there for my sister and me. She loved us deeply. My sister and I often got into fights before my mom got home from work. She'd walk in the door and we'd start whining and explaining who really started the fight. Mom couldn't figure out who was telling the truth or bear to think she was punishing the wrong child so she'd paddle us both. The paddle was labeled, *Heat for the seat*. Every time she spanked us, she'd say "You two need to behave. I have to work and I can't worry about you. I love you and I don't like paddling you." I always felt worse about upsetting her than the paddling itself.

My mom stayed with my dad because she didn't feel like she had any options. She was doing her best to earn a living at K-Mart but she knew she couldn't raise two children on her income. By the time I was ten, things at home were getting worse. My parents fought and fought. My sister was 15 and couldn't wait to turn 18 so she could move out and get a job. I decided I would join the military and move out as soon as possible. I remember one particularly terrible fight. My dad was throwing things, screaming and raging through the house. My sister was screaming in her room with the door locked. My mom came into my room and climbed into bed with me. "It's going to be OK Grady; he's just upset," she repeated over and over as she snuggled up to me.

My dad walked into my bedroom, screamed, spit in my mom's face and slapped the fire out of her. I came unglued on the inside. I thought about my dad's shotgun and realized I didn't know where it was. My sister jumped out her bedroom window and ran down the street screaming for help. My mom laid on the bed and through her tears was telling me that it was going to be OK. My dad went to their bedroom to lie down. I jumped up, grabbed my baseball bat and went into his room and hit him in the shins. He came up out of the bed looking like the Hulk. He snatched me up and beat me so badly that I couldn't sit down at school the next day. The welts bled for days.

I hated my father for being gone so much, for drinking, for his nickname "El Studo", for beating me but most of all for hurting my mother. My mom was the constant in our family through these tough years. She was always ready to listen and always encouraging us in our disappointments and failures. She was not one to give out advice; she just covered everything in love. She was one tough woman. She never said a bad word to me about my father. She constantly assured me that he loved me and that everything was going to turn out all right. I don't know how she did it but she did. She covered everything she did in love.

"Grady, why do you want to write that book?" Mom would ask me. Because people need to hear my story. So they can forgive their fathers just like I forgave mine or maybe even forgive themselves. I want them to know that grace is there for the asking. People make mistakes, terrible mistakes. Forgiveness is possible. God can help you forgive others and yourself.

She smiles, "Just don't call me Granny in your book because I'm your mother!" I call her granny all the time so I might get "the heat" for writing that.

Fatherless

I meet so many young men and women who have grown up without a father. Absent men and lonely mothers, grinding it out day after day for the sake of their children. They sacrifice everything for their children without the help of the man who wanted to sow the seed but refused to stay and help maintain the garden.

I believe every child needs a father. It took a man to conceive the child and it takes a man to raise the child. I hate looking into the eyes of children and seeing the hurt, loss and emptiness caused by an absent dad. God can meet needs and heal hurts but these children need a daddy!

Moms can do it alone, but it wasn't set up to be that way. God intended there to be three main people responsible for the raising of children: God, mom and dad. *"A three-stranded rope isn't easily snapped."* Ecclesiastes 4:12.

There are plenty of single moms with a man sitting on the couch. I'm so sick of this crap. I just want to give these suckers the right hand of fellowship. They go to work everyday, bring home a paycheck and then settle into their captain's chair. "Why are these kids running around? Why is this house a mess? Why can't I just watch a little TV in peace and quiet? Where's my dinner?" they think.

Well this part of the book is for you, fool! While you are at work, there's a mama at home taking care of your seed, loving your kids and running them here and there. She gets them involved in sports because you don't have time to be a father. If they are playing a sport, she knows a coach might see something in them and give them the attention and guidance they need from a man.

The real work begins when you come home. Stop whining about your day and leave it at the door. Put your captain's chair on the corner for the trash truck to pick up. Sit down on the floor and play with your kids or sit down at the table with them. Show them some love. Your attention might keep them from running around trying to get any kind of attention they can, good or bad. I looked for attention by being the class clown. I was a living example of what a boy will do to get the attention he isn't getting from his daddy. I'm so thankful for all my coaches who picked me up and dropped me off after practice and even invited me to their homes for cookouts.

There are some men who are stepping up to the plate and acting like fathers. Many are not. Don't hide behind excuses like, "I'm tired, I need my space or I need a guys night out every day of the week." No. You need to get on your knees and tell the woman who birthed your kids you love her and want to help. "Baby, let me cook dinner or take the kids to the park or a game." I know its Saturday and your favorite sport is on, but the only game that really needs playing, the one that is the most important to win, is the one you're not even playing; being a daddy.

If you're reading this book and your father was abusive or absent, there's healing for you. Jesus is the ultimate father. He's always present and available. If you're a dad and you weren't there for your children when they were younger, do everything you can to go after them now. On the outside they may look ok, but on the inside they're still carrying scars and hurts from the past. Talk to them. Ask their forgiveness. Tell them you love them and want things to be different.

Thank your moms for always loving us and wrapping their arms around us when we need it. Thank you for seeing me as a child and not a mistake. Thank you for believing in me when the road was rough. Thank you for never giving up on me. Even as an orphan my mom knew what it meant to love.

I love you Mom.

Forgiveness

The rest of the story.

My granddad passed away suddenly in 1980. His last audible words were a prayer for my dad, "God meet him and help him see himself as You see him."

My dad got the news on the road that his dad was close to dying, dropped his cargo off and headed home. When he arrived home, he sat down in the kitchen and wept uncontrollably. I sat at his feet with my arms wrapped around his legs and said, "Dad, what's wrong?" My mom told me that my granddad just died. I ran to my room, buried my head in a pillow and cried. I was so hurt to see my dad cry because he was always so strong.

Dad never spoke with me about his father's death. He lived quietly with his grief. He loved his dad but because of my dad's lifestyle, he kept a distance from his dad to avoid getting *preached to*. The grief ate at him. He wore dark sunglasses constantly for four years. He came to family gatherings but never took his glasses off. He had so much pain inside. His eyes were black from lack of sleep.

In 1981 my dad was unloading huge bails of cotton at RJ Reynolds Tobacco Company in Winston Salem, NC. Each bail weighed about 1500 pounds. He was pulling the tarps off when a forklift driver accidentally nudged one of the bails. It rolled off the trailer and pinned my dad to the ground. It took ten men working together to roll the bail off his chest. He didn't have a pulse for two minutes while one guy pounded his chest repeatedly. When my dad woke up, all he could remember was seeing bright lights.

He was rushed to the hospital where we learned that he had several broken ribs and was badly bruised. Two days later when he was released from the hospital, he said he felt he had been given a second chance at life. He began to go to church and for the first time, we went together.

About a year later my dad started a small trucking company and his stress was even worse than when he drove a truck. I have a lot of respect for the men and women who provide the service that puts goods on our shelves and I certainly wouldn't want to be a truck driver or own a trucking company. Folks who have those jobs are overworked and underpaid. My dad carried so much stress from running his business that he had a heart attack in 1988. He decided to sell his business and go back on the road driving a big rig. Oh boy! This time around he did things differently. He bought his dream truck that was chromed out and lit up like a Christmas tree. It even came with a walk-in sleeper. He was so proud of that truck. He changed his CB handle to *Honest Abe* with whom he shared a birthday and was back on the road again.

Things at home were not perfect but greatly improved. He stopped drinking and his temper quieted down. I was 16, busy with school and sports, but inside I still needed a daddy. He did make an effort to be home on the weekends and go to church. I was still hurting and angry from our past and it was special to sit next to him and sing, *Just a Little Talk with Jesus* from page 92 in the red hymnal. How that chorus moved me.

"Now let us have a little talk with Jesus
Let us tell Him all about our troubles
He will hear our faintest cry
He will answer by and by
Now when you feel a little prayer wheel turning
And you know a little fire is burning
You will find a little talk with Jesus makes it right."

My Aunt Ann was in charge of planning the music for Sunday services and I'd beg her to include that hymn every Sunday. My dad loved the hymn, *Just as I Am*. I'd watch the tears flow down his face as he sang the words, *welcome pardon, cleanse, relieve, because thy promise I believe*. Even though I knew he was receiving pardon from God, he didn't know how to say he was sorry to me. He never *said* he was sorry during his life but he lived out his regret and learned to love me better. He accepted and cared for me when I showed up on his doorstep.

I've learned that forgiveness isn't just for the other person; it's for you as well. You don't need to wait on someone else to forgive you because that is their journey and this is your journey. You'll be released when you let go of the anger you hold onto by denying forgiveness.

Pain

Sometimes life just seems to twist you up in knots. "God, why would you put me through this to then take me out of it? Why not just take me down another road? Why even get pregnant just to miscarry? Why give me a child to then take him or her away? Why give me a ministry and then take it away?" I'll tell ya! Sometimes God uses pain to show us things we wouldn't see on the scenic route. He'll take you down the back country roads, dirty and so bumpy you'll blow your tires out, bust up your windshield and mess up your front grill. It'll be rough.

God's journey for you won't be the one you planned for yourself. He'll put you here and there. There'll be days when you'll ask, why? You'll find yourself in places asking, "How does this line up with the call?" I believe every living minute is His plan for your life. Don't look around; just keep your hand on the plow and your eye on the prize! What prize? Jesus. Philippians 3: 12-14 spells it out:

Philippians 3: 12-14
"I'm not saying that I have this all together, that I have it made. But I am well on my way, reaching out for Christ, who has so wondrously reached out for me. Friends, don't get me wrong: By no means do I count myself an expert in all of this, but I've got my eye on the goal, where God is beckoning us onward—to Jesus. I'm off and running and I'm not turning back."

Endurance
Sixteen weeks of Parris Island, South Carolina will make any Marine recruit wonder why they signed up. I arrived at

boot camp sitting on a crowded bus with a drill instructor's veins popping out of his head as he clambered up the steps barking like a bulldog. Smokey Bear, (the name for a Drill Instructor's Hat for those unfamiliar with the Marine lingo), was cocked down on his forehead and he was wearing a uniform that looked like it had just come from the cleaners. He screamed in his raspy and low bulldog voice, "When I give you the command to move, you'll get off my bus. Do you understand?" "Yes sir!" we screamed. "You put your nasty feet on those yellow foot prints and lock your body," he yelled.

I went into the Marines for all the wrong reasons. I didn't want to hear what my daddy had to say about becoming a man, didn't want to go college, didn't want to get a job and get into a rut in life. I decided to go into the military. I had two uncles who were in the Army. My Uncle Harvey Lloyd, whom I looked up to as a child, was a retired drill instructor. I also have a cousin who went into the Marines. He's the biggest son of gun you'll ever meet. Every kid in our family loves Leroy Lunsford...he's a haus!

I thought if I went into the Navy, I'd always wonder what it would be like to be a Marine. So I went right into the recruiter's office and said, "I'm ready to go. When can I leave?" Someone from the recruiter's office called my house sixty days later and my dad answered the phone. "Mr. Shope, we'd like to speak with Grady." My dad told him that I was out working with my cousins. "Well, tell him he leaves for the Marine Corp boot camp in the morning." My parents didn't know I signed up. It was two o'clock in the afternoon and my dad was looking for me while my mom was freaking out. I guess you could say they weren't proud of me at that moment.

I'm sitting about halfway back on the bus, thinking to myself, "When this bulldog tells me to move, I'm coming off this bus." He screamed, "Get off my bus!" I went across those seats, stepping on people, shoving and running for the front. Recruits were going in every direction. Some even jumped out of the emergency exit windows. I ran to the front and put my feet on those yellow foot prints. With the drill instructor screaming in our faces, I was going to be first and didn't care what everybody else was doing.

I stood at attention on those footprints screaming at the top of my lungs, "Yes Sir! Yes sir! Yes Sir!" Move here, move there. Do this, do that. They marched us straight to the barber for a free haircut and our hair was gone in about 30 seconds. It's amazing how quickly everyone started to look alike. Long hair, gone. Short hair gone. Flat top, gone.

It's midnight. They've shaved our heads, shoved gear at us and herded us like cattle. We are exhausted from no sleep, scared to death and homesick. "We're going to give you ten seconds to let you girls write your mama a letter," as pencil and paper were being passed around. I wrote four words, "Please come get me." That's exactly what my letter to my mom said. As funny as that is today, I was serious. I wanted off that island.

Have you ever seen someone harm themselves to get back at someone else? Someone gets drunk because they're mad at their spouse. They're trying to hurt someone but they end up hurting themselves. That was me. I joined up to avoid my dad but also prove to him I was a man. Now I was begging, "Please come get me."

Days passed and no one came to my rescue. I got a letter from my dad and my thought was that I didn't write my dad, I wrote my mother. Sometimes even when we don't want to, we need to hear what our dad has to say. His letter said, "If you don't graduate then don't come home, dad." Ladies and gentlemen, I stayed and endured sixteen weeks of hell. I didn't enjoy it but I had to go through it and I came out the other side stronger. Our heavenly Father may engineer circumstances or allow circumstances that are anything but what we want but He is with us. "And we know that in all things God works for the good of those who love him," Romans 8:28.

On December 19, 1990, I put on the finest uniform with flawless brass and my shoes were shining. I peeled my shoulders back and graduated with Platoon 3119. "Thump'n 3rd" we were called. Those Marine Dress Blues are the most spectacular uniforms in the world. My mother walked right by me on the field. "Mom," I said. She turned around and said, "Oh my gosh, what did they do to my baby?" Those might be the first words of every Marine mother when they meet their son after boot camp.

My dad came to my graduation but I was only interested in seeing my mom and girlfriend. My anger was like a wall of sadness from my childhood memories. I could tell he was proud and wanted to be closer to me but the wall was just too thick. My dad shook my hand and looked me up and down and said, "Congratulations, you did it." As good as I looked on the outside; I was still hurting on the inside.

I finished my tour with the Marines and returned to Asheville, NC. I didn't visit my dad much even though we lived in the same town. My mom told me that my dad just didn't know how to engage with me because I was so distant with him. I couldn't even bring myself to meet him for lunch.

Prophecy

Fast forward to 2001. I was in full-time ministry and trying to find my way as I traveled around the world. One of the most profound moments in my life was about to take place. I attended a men's conference in Spartanburg, SC where a man by the name of Ferguson McIntyre was the guest speaker. He was Australian and reminded me of a big teddy bear. "Love God and love people," he said over and over with his Aussie accent.

One evening as I sat mid way back in a room of about 250 men, he walked right up to me and said, "Grady, come here!" He looked into my eyes and said, "You've got a lot of hurt inside you towards your father." Oh my, I thought.

I have suppressed all that mess and it's deep, deep down inside. "You need to forgive your father and make things right." I sank to the floor and began to cry.

"Men, this one has been called. Watch him. Not only will he write books but people will write books about him!" I left the conference thinking about those words McIntyre spoke over me, wondering if it was real or some sort of dream. Well, here I am. I've forgiven my dad and I'm writing my first book. I think I have several more in me!

Reconciliation

The next day I was driving home in my 500 SEL Mercedes Benz. Yes, I like cars too. That car was my pride and joy. Nicest car I've owned in my life. Driving up Saluda Mountain with the sun in my face, I pulled over to find my sunglasses. Sitting there, I felt like God was saying, "I want you to give this car to your dad as an act of forgiveness." I was like, what?

When I feel like God wants me to give something or do something, I just do it. It weighs on me if I don't. I'm so blessed today from being obedient. Never think God can't use the little you have because He's just looking for a vessel to pour Himself through. I could write a whole book on this alone and maybe one day I will.

I drove straight to my daddy's house, pulled up and said, "I've got something for you." He came to the car and I handed the keys to him. He said, "No way Son." I replied, "I don't look that good in it. I look like a pimp. You've got the class and smoothness to pull it off." He couldn't believe it.

That would be the last car my dad would own for the rest of his life. He looked so good behind that wheel. He would pull up in the car, roll his window down and say, "I do look better than you!" I found out how liberating forgiving someone could be. I felt free to build a relationship with my dad that we had never had and we did.

In 1993 my dad had a terrible accident. He was driving his rig and was just 100 yards from his house when he had a massive heart attack and ran off the road. My mom called me as EMS took him to the hospital. I helped oversee the tow trucks and talked to the police as they pulled his rig away. I picked up some personal items from his house to take to the hospital. Even in my pain, he was still my daddy as I picked up his shaving kit, wallet and Bible. I just wanted him to say he was sorry and proud. I carried his things to the emergency room and my mom said she thought he was going to be OK but he had a long road ahead of him.

The doctor put in a pace maker and an internal defibrillator. To his dying day, he thanked God for Dr. William T. Maddox, Jr., the man who saved his life. He loved that man.

A New Heart

My dad volunteered over 13,000 hours in the heart center of Memorial Mission Hospital and was known to many people during the last years of his life. He counseled people who were scheduled to receive internal defibrillators and families who had a loved one in surgery. The hospital would page him daily to talk to a specific patient. Because he was a volunteer, he made his own rules. Sounds like what a Shope would do.

He would pray for everyone he met and even atheists asked him to pray. His greatest honor during his time at the hospital was praying for Ruth Graham, the late wife of Rev. Billy Graham. The last will be first. God redeemed that man who beat his kids, laid out drunk, slapped his wife and ran reckless for years. The one whose daddy prayed for him on his deathbed.

The devil will spend a lifetime beating you up and trying to find a way to steal God's call for your life. But God's specialty is working with the scraps. He doesn't need fancy suits and high dollar shoes. He wants the one who's been overlooked, the one you thought wouldn't make it, the one eating the crumbs from the master's table, the one who failed, the one nobody wants to talk to and the one you wished would have killed himself.

God doesn't throw away the Scraps, He uses them!

This is it!

I'm finishing a chapter of my life and God is beginning to write the next.

Through all the mess of the past seven years, God has done some amazing things in my life. To think God isn't present in our lives is a lie from hell. Even when doors were slammed in my face, God still had a plan. Don't let what the enemy has stolen from you keep you down. God has His plan and He will redeem the difficult things in your life.

2 x 4's

In 2004 I had a really good friend encourage me to become a General Contractor but I explained that I knew nothing about building. I didn't even know which end of a 2x4 to grab. "Grady, you've got good leadership skills, manage people well and you understand money." For someone who was broke, busted and couldn't be trusted, those words seemed ridiculous. On the other hand, what did I have to lose? In March 2005 I passed the State General Contractors Exam. I walked out of the test center and called my dad. "Hey, I'm a General Contractor now." "You know nothing about building," he replied.

God didn't put me in a place I knew well. He invited me to step out of the boat, to leave my comfort zone and try something new. Did I ever step out of the boat! Even when our lives are in turmoil, God has a purpose. I built four new homes in one year and was encouraged to pursue commercial construction. It was fast and exciting. Buying land, building beautiful homes and seeing families move in was awesome. I was working 80 to 100 hours a week.

My dad taught me how to work. I'd play a Friday night high school football game and get home late. I was tired and bruised and have only one thought on my mind, "I'm sleeping in tomorrow." My dad was tossing me out bed at 6am. "Time to get at it Bo." I hated Saturdays! Today I'm thankful for the work ethic he taught me. I get up most days at 4:30 am and by 7:00 am have gotten more done than many people do all day. *Thanks Dad!*

Shawn

Working as a contractor I tried to spend as much time with my son as I could. When kids get their drivers license it's hard to pin them down but when they need some gas money, they'll find you. It's like they have GPS on you. Don't you love it when you're trying to get in touch with them and they won't answer the phone but will send a text that reads, "What's up?" I text back and say, "*What's up* better answer that phone."

One Friday night, as my son and I were walking out of a movie theater, we walked past an old friend of mine. "Hey Grady!" My son, Kelby said, "Dad, I think someone is trying to get your attention." Her name was Shawn. We chatted for a minute. She asked how I was doing and I told her that I was separated. She said she divorced years ago and life was good. We didn't exchange numbers and she and her girlfriend went into the movie theater as Kelby and I went our way. "She seems nice," Kelby said. "Yeah, but she's got kids." "So do you! Duh!" he laughed.

The next day my cell phone started beeping, "You've got a message." I ignored it because I thought it was a scam or virus. Finally I asked one my construction guys about the message alert on my phone. "It's a text," he explained. I know you're thinking that I'm behaving like I was living in the 1970's but I thought if someone wanted to talk to me, they should call me! The text was from Shawn. "It was good to see you last night; let's get together sometime." I had to get the same guy that told me it was a text to text her back. I wondered how she got my number and she said I had given her a business card about a year ago and she put it in her night stand. What? I didn't even remember seeing her. She says I acted like a fruit loop when she saw me out. It must've been one of those days.

We started hanging out and I made it clear that we could only be friends because I still had hopes of restoring my marriage. I told her the whole story and she thought I was crazy but I wanted to believe that reconciliation could happen. I hadn't had contact with my wife for years but I thought perhaps God would work a miracle.

I hung out with Shawn, my son and her girls. Things seemed really cool. Man, could she cook! I'm the size of a dump truck. One thing for certain is that we didn't miss any meals. It's that sneaky weapon women have to win a man's heart through his stomach. Men can be so gullible. "Nah, we're just friends; nothing happening here," as you wipe the gravy off your shirt. It's a weapon, men, beware.

"If you want your marriage to work, I will offer to go to her church and wait after the service to talk to her," Shawn volunteered. "She's crazy not to reconcile with you because you're a great person. You are not the person people from that church say you are." I was shocked she would even think to say this to me. My dad was waiting up for me when I got home from my evening with Shawn.

I was 34 years old, living with my dad and he said, "In by ten or must be sin." My dad still had rules for me even at the age of 34! "How was your day?" he questioned. "Good, and an interesting evening with Shawn." "Oh yeah, what's up?" I told him what she suggested she would do and he looked me at me like I had ten heads. "What, Dad?" "I understand you want reconciliation, but son, you're chasing the wrong woman."

I needed closure with my wife and didn't want to start a new relationship until God closed the door or worked some kind of miracle. Months went by. Shawn remained a good friend. My wife filed for divorce. Our only contact was through an attorney and it had been almost eighteen months since the last time I saw her. I was served divorce papers and 30 days later at nine am she was in court alone. I went to work that day and kept believing that God might give her a change of heart.

Months later I walked into my real estate attorney's office to close on a piece of property and my now ex-wife was walking out. I was relieved to get to talk to her alone, just the two of us. Standing in the hall for fifteen minutes, I listened to her explain why she wouldn't reconcile or even communicate with me. The only thing I really heard from that conversation was, "When I married you, there was no emotion." Wow! Talk about dropping a bomb on somebody. I was so shocked I could've kissed a donkey on the mouth.

Don't think for a minute that hearing that didn't hurt a little. God ordained that meeting because I needed closure and He didn't just shut that door, He slammed it. It was so emotional for me. I felt like a Mack truck had been lifted off me. I didn't know what to do with myself. I wanted to go run down the interstate. It was the key that unlocked everything. I got in my truck and called Shawn to tell her what happened. "Great, you hungry?" There it is a again, that sneaky weapon.

Later that day I told my dad what happened. "It's about time you divorced her because she divorced you months ago." How many times in life have we held on to something that's not there and the whole time God had the real deal right in front of us? You lost that job and the new job was right there. You couldn't buy that car because God had a better one. You had to move out of that house because He had something better in mind. I don't mean bigger, more expensive or more luxurious; I mean better for you. God knows what His children need. God took what the devil had stolen from me, gave something else back and then some. He took the bad in my life and turned it into good.

Here comes the Holy Spirit, so hold on. Buckle your seatbelts because this is going to be a ride. I'm tired of priming the pump so let's just get right to it. Let me lay this down.

Shew! I get excited when people tell me about their problems because it gives me the opportunity to tell them about the solution. Welcome God into your life and He'll fix it up. The world hands out disappointment and God hands out life. He'll move mountains in your life. He just wants you to let Him in. I can't start preaching yet because I need to tell you the rest of the story.

Nine months later in March 2007, Shawn and I went to New York City for the St. Patrick's Day parade. I love New

York City and I wanted to share it with the woman who had become such a great friend to me. She also fed me well for the past two years! I wanted to bless her socks off. I also had a big surprise planned.

We arrived in New York, checked into our hotel and went exploring. It began to snow as we walked into central park. I hired a horse and buggy and asked the guy to take us to the lake. Off we went. When we arrived I asked the driver to take our picture. As he aimed the camera our way, I got on one knee in the snow and asked my best friend to marry me. She said, "I'm hungry." Na! She said, "Yes!" Those big beautiful blue eyes sparkled in the snow.

The parade was the next day and I wanted us to have a good spot. Shawn is Irish and I love the bands, especially the bagpipes. I was so excited to share this with her.

Walking down Fifth Avenue we were approached by a gentleman who said, "Hey, where are you from?" As soon as I opened my mouth and started to answer, he leaned in and laughed, "You guys from the south?" "Yes sir," I replied. "My name is Dr. Dan and I'm a reporter from a local radio station." Shawn began to tell him about the wonderful evening we had enjoyed and showed him her ring.

He paused and then said, "How would you like to be blessed by the Cardinal?" At this point I'm thinking, this *IS* New York City. I've visited the Big Apple at least twenty times and people can come up with amazing ways to take advantage of tourists. "Sure," I said sarcastically. "Here's my card," he said. "Call me when the parade starts and I'll come get you."

We walked off and I said to Shawn, "Whatever!" We watched the parade for about 30 minutes and I said, "Let's see if we can get near St. Patrick's Cathedral since the performers will stop there for a performance because it'll be on National TV." We tried to get close to the Cathedral but the crowd was at least 40 people deep. It was insane. I got ole' Dr. Dan's card out and dialed the number.

I was surprised when he answered. "Hey, I'm in front of the cathedral but it's 40 people deep." "What street?" he asked. I told him where we were. Out of no where, people started parting and here comes the NYPD and Dr. Dan. I looked at Shawn, "Let's go!" We started walking towards them and

Dr. Dan said, "Where have you been?" I had no response. Everyone was looking at us wondering who we were. We finally made it to the street and four police officers escorted us to steps of the cathedral. We were shocked. Knowing national TV was rolling, I called my dad and told him to look for us. He was laughing as I hung up with, "I'll explain later."

Now we were enjoying the parade from the front row. I was in awe. Dr. Dan said, "I talked to the Cardinal and he wants to bless you guys." Speechless and with tears in my eyes, I thought, God, your word is so true, the last will be first. What the devil stole, God was ordaining on national television. With the cameras rolling, the cardinal came and prayed for Shawn and me. He declared grace and peace over our lives. "May nothing tear apart the thing God ordained. Always love each other in everything you do," he said as he looked at us.

Local TV stations interviewed us and when the parade was over, we left and went to eat at Carnegie Deli. Later that night we watched ourselves on the eleven o'clock news. My dad called to tell us how happy he was for us.

Four months later we got married with over 300 friends and family supporting us. Today I'm so blessed with two beautiful step-daughters, Jordan and Alli, my awesome son Kelby and the most beautiful person in the world, my wife Shawn. She's my friend, my cheerleader, my fighter and the one who saw something in the scraps. And man she can cook, have I told you that?

Full Steam Ahead

I was going to quit and was planning my exit when God started teaching me that He can use the discarded, broken and messed up. There was nothing left to my faith but a tiny ember. I thought God couldn't use me anymore. The devil is evil and deceitful and breathing lies down our necks like *useless and worthless*.

After church one Sunday I stood in our kitchen and told Shawn, "Baby, fill the boiler." She looked at me and said, "What?" "I feel like a steam locomotive. I've waited for this day and that tiny ember is ready to be stoked to power this train. Grab the shovel! I want to tell my story for somebody who feels there is no second chance for them; for somebody who feels grace isn't for them and for someone who feels there's no hope."

I thought my ministry was dead and that every door had shut. I thought I was *book shelved* and my voice silenced and that my life wasn't worth continuing. The same God who brought me into this world is the same God that is about ready to kick the door open and bring me out. This isn't just for me, it's for you!

My wife, my cheerleader, my right hand, the one that encouraged and cared for me, said, "Honey, when you got free, the whole house got free." She explained how my freedom in grace had changed the entire atmosphere of our home. "Go for it!" she encouraged.

Praise God and listen up!

God is pulling for you and fanning that ember deep inside of you, inviting you into the freedom He has waiting for you. You can't have us, devil! You won't take our families, our ministries and our relationships with God. You'll have to take your circus somewhere else. Come on folks, it's a fight! Don't give up.

You may feel like you're moving backwards, but it takes time. While the coal is getting shoveled in, it is building up steam that will be released little by little. The train wants to move, the wheels are trying to grip the track, they slip a little more and the train loses its momentum and starts to roll back. People on the outside think that ole train is done; that it's too rusty; that it's been buried and nobody wants it. They see it rolling back and think, *no, no, no.* It's just trying to get its grip, so put some more coal on the fire, baby, because this train is getting ready to roll.

I know it appears that the devil has the brake on your train but the devil can't take your life unless you allow it. I'm coming to get what the devil stole and wreck his house. No more will you steal my family, my ministry and my relationship with God. Devil, I hope you have a dental plan because I'm about to kick your teeth in.

That's right. I'm in the ring and taking the gloves off this time because it's a fight!

I'm coming and this time I'm bringing the whole family. Kelby, release the brake son. Jordan, wave, because we're about to leave the station and Alli, get your game face on, sound the horn and baby, keep shoveling the coal. We're going full steam ahead because you messed with the wrong family and it's a fight.

Shew! Don't ever think for one minute you're finished. As my dad often said, "If you're breathing the air of this world God isn't finished."

Thank you God for never giving up on me. Lord, I ask that my story will challenge and encourage anyone who reads my book! May it be a piece of the puzzle they need for healing, freedom and to know that grace is for them.

God is in the reconciliation business. You might be scraps, but God uses the scraps.

Blessings, W. Grady Shope

"Hang in there, like a hair in a biscuit"

16735468R00060

Made in the USA
Charleston, SC
08 January 2013